RIPPLES!

black hole

$$\left[\nabla^2 - \frac{1}{c^2}\frac{\partial^2}{\partial t^2}\right]h_{\mu\nu} = 0$$

stee
flou

$$G_{\mu\nu} = \frac{8\pi G}{c^4}T_{\mu\nu}$$

light waves hit the light detector

Beam splitter

$T = 0.5\%$

LIGO

$$h = \frac{2G}{c^4}\frac{1}{r}\frac{\partial^2 Q}{\partial t^2}$$

light-storage photo protector.

$$G_{\mu\nu} = \frac{8\pi G}{c^4}T_{\mu\nu}$$

GW
read out

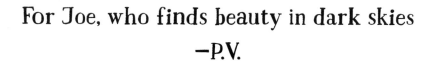

For Joe, who finds beauty in dark skies
—P.V.

Text copyright © 2022 by Patricia Valdez
Jacket art and interior illustrations copyright © 2022 by Sara Palacios

All rights reserved. Published in the United States by Alfred A. Knopf, an imprint of
Random House Children's Books, a division of Penguin Random House LLC, New York.

Knopf, Borzoi Books, and the colophon are registered trademarks of Penguin Random House LLC.

Visit us on the Web! rhcbooks.com
Educators and librarians, for a variety of teaching tools, visit us at RHTeachersLibrarians.com

Library of Congress Cataloging-in-Publication Data is available upon request.
ISBN 978-1-9848-9459-5 (trade) — ISBN 978-1-9848-9460-1 (lib. bdg.) — ISBN 978-1-9848-9461-8 (ebook)

The text of this book is set in 15-point Serifa.
The illustrations were created using watercolors and digital media.
Book design by Elizabeth Tardiff

MANUFACTURED IN CHINA
March 2022
10 9 8 7 6 5 4 3 2 1
First Edition

HOW TO HEAR THE UNIVERSE

Gaby González and the Search for Einstein's Ripples in Space-Time

by Patricia Valdez

illustrated by Sara Palacios

Alfred A. Knopf
New York

About a hundred years ago,
in the German city of Berlin,
a scientist named Albert Einstein searched for the
secrets of the universe.

First, his thoughts turned to motion, time, and space.

Everything in the universe moves through space.

A dragonfly, for example, darts . . .

forward and backward,

side to side,

and up and down.

$$h = \frac{2G}{c^4} \frac{1}{r} \frac{\partial^2 Q}{\partial t^2}$$

As the dragonfly moves through space, time passes. Einstein understood that space and time are linked together, weaving an invisible fabric around the dragonfly. For that reason, the dragonfly doesn't just move through space; it moves through the fabric of space-time.

$$= \frac{8\pi G}{c^4} T_{\alpha\beta}$$

$$\left[\nabla^2 - \frac{1}{c^2} \frac{\partial^2}{\partial t^2} \right] h_{\mu\nu} = 0$$

Next, Einstein's thoughts turned to gravity.

Gravity pulls things down toward Earth. It keeps a resting dragonfly from floating off into space.

Gravity also keeps the Earth and other planets in orbit around the sun.

Einstein wondered what caused gravity.

He questioned,

predicted,

and calculated.

Until he arrived at a beautiful solution:

Gravity is caused by the curving of space-time around large objects.

Just as a lily pad curves underneath a frog, space-time curves around the Earth.

If the frog on the lily pad jumps up and down, the energy from the jumps causes ripples throughout the lily pad.

Einstein wondered if energy from colliding stars could cause ripples in space-time.

He returned to his calculations.

The following year, Einstein announced that space-time could indeed ripple.

$$\left[\nabla^2 - \frac{1}{c^2} \right]$$

$$G_{\alpha\beta} = \frac{8\pi G}{c^4} T_{\alpha\beta}$$

$$h = \frac{2G}{c^4} \frac{1}{r}$$

But he concluded that the ripples would never be detected. They would be much too faint to hear by the time they reached Earth.

Without a way to hear ripples in space-time, people considered Einstein's idea simply a fairy tale.

About fifty years later,

on a warm night in Argentina,

beneath the moon, the stars, and the sky,

a young girl named Gaby González looked up.

She, too, wondered what secrets lay beyond the stars.

Each year, Gaby and her family went camping. Far away from the city, the stars shone brighter. And Gaby's curiosity grew deeper.

In school, Gaby learned about physics. The science of energy and motion attracted her like a magnet. Gaby thought physics could help answer her questions about the universe, just as Einstein had.

When she went to college, Gaby learned about Einstein's ripples in space-time. Scientists had tried for many years to find them.

But they only heard background noise from crashing waves,

gusting winds, and passing trucks.

Ripples in space-time remained just an idea.

After college, Gaby moved from sunny Córdoba, Argentina, to snowy Syracuse, New York. There, she worked on ways to better understand space-time.

Gaby found her new world exciting. When she missed her family and friends in Argentina, she imagined they were all connected by space-time.

Soon Gaby met a new professor working on hearing ripples in space-time. She leapt at the opportunity to help hear the distant universe. With his help, Gaby set out to tackle the problem of background noise.

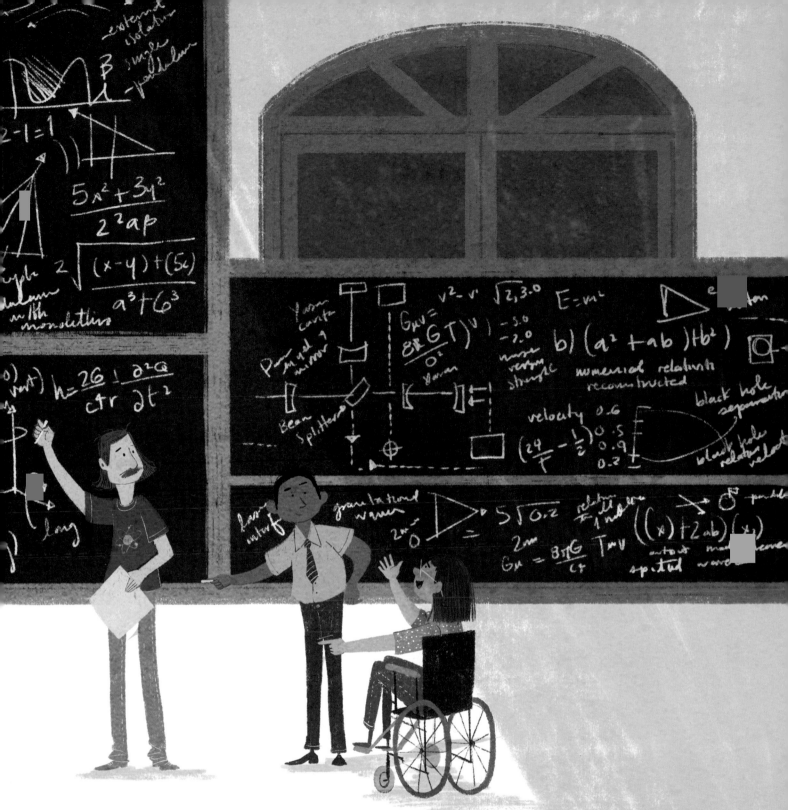

She spent long days and long nights
thinking,
testing,
and measuring.
Gaby's work brought the world one step closer to space-time.

By this time, scientists were ready to build two big machines called LIGO, which would help detect space-time ripples. One would be built in Hanford, Washington, and the other in Livingston, Louisiana.

The LIGO project needed experts to help predict and remove background noise.

Lucky for LIGO, Gaby was ready. As her team learned to predict different kinds of background noises, LIGO became even better at hearing faint signals.

Years passed, and the LIGO team grew to include over a thousand people across the world. Finally, it was time for LIGO to begin its search for ripples in space-time. But first, Gaby's group needed to make sure that background noise wouldn't keep them from hearing the ripples.

They created different noises to see how LIGO reacted. They stomped, rattled, and rolled, running tests late into the night.

The team decided to finish the tests the next morning, so they left the instrument on overnight.

Suddenly, in the early morning, the LIGO Livingston detector chirped. The LIGO Hanford detector chirped seven milliseconds later.

The next day, Gaby awoke to an alert from LIGO.

Could it be?

Right away, Gaby and her team studied the waves that LIGO detected. They measured and re-measured,

calculated and re-calculated,

analyzed and re-analyzed,

until they were certain of what they had found:

ripples in space-time caused by the collision of two black holes!

A long time ago, in the distant universe, two black holes circled each other, moving faster and faster, until they collided to form a larger black hole. The energy released caused space-time to ripple, just like the collision of the frog and lily pad causes ripples. Those ripples moved toward Earth over time, and more than a billion years later, they passed through LIGO.

One hundred years after Einstein's prediction,

Gaby and her LIGO team proved him right.

With a new way to hear the universe,

we can now uncover its secrets,

one ripple at a time.

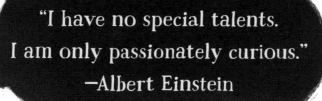

"I have no special talents.
I am only passionately curious."
—Albert Einstein

Albert Einstein's Theory of General Relativity

Albert Einstein published his Theory of General Relativity in 1915. His theory explained that gravity was not simply a force that attracted objects, like Sir Isaac Newton's apple falling from a tree to the ground. Instead, Einstein explained that gravity was the result of a distortion, or curvature, of space-time caused by a large mass, or dense object. Space-time can be imagined as a large lily pad. A heavy frog sitting on the lily pad would cause it to curve. A pebble placed on the lily pad would move toward the frog because of the curvature of the lily pad. Like the frog, our sun curves space-time, and the planets follow the curve in an orbit around the sun.

Einstein further predicted that when two massive objects like neutron stars circle each other and collide, the energy produced would be strong enough to create ripples in space-time, like ripples on a pond. He concluded that these ripples, called gravitational waves, would be impossible to detect because of how small the signals would become by the time they reached Earth.

"We want to know everything about the universe—that's humanity. We are very, very curious."
—Gabriela González

Gabriela González and the Detection of Gravitational Waves (Ripples in Space-Time)

Gabriela (Gaby) González was born on February 24, 1965, in Córdoba, Argentina. She studied physics at the University of Córdoba and earned her PhD from the University of Syracuse. As a graduate student, Gaby worked with Peter R. Saulson on the challenge of predicting thermal noise, a type of background sound caused by the tiniest parts of the detector itself—its own atoms! Gaby eventually joined Louisiana State University (LSU) and became the first female full professor in the physics department. She trained young scientists to ask *Why?*

From 2011 to 2017, Gaby served as the spokesperson for the LIGO Scientific Collaboration. On September 14, 2015, LIGO detected its first gravitational wave (GW150914), produced by a collision of two black holes 1.3 billion years ago. As the LIGO spokesperson, Gaby was part of the team that announced, to much fanfare, the discovery of gravitational waves, on February 11, 2016. In 2017, González was awarded the Bruno Rossi Prize from the American Astronomical Society and the National Academy of Sciences Award for Scientific Discovery. She was elected to the American Academy of Arts and Sciences that same year. González is a professor of physics at LSU, where she and her group study the detection of gravitational waves. González was promoted to Boyd Professor in 2019, the highest professorial rank awarded by LSU. Her husband, Jorge Pullin, is a professor of theoretical physics at LSU.

More About LIGO

The Laser Interferometer Gravitational-Wave Observatory, or LIGO, has two arms, each over two miles long, that form an L-shape. Laser beams travel down each arm and are reflected by mirrors at the end of the tunnels. When the beams arrive back at the start, the light waves interfere with, or cancel out each other, so no light is detected. Gravitational waves stretch and shrink space-time as they move through the universe. Likewise, once the waves reach LIGO, they stretch and shrink the two arms, and the light beams traveling through the tunnels no longer cancel each other out. Thus, light travels to the detector, and an event is registered.

Since the first detection, LIGO has gone on to detect even more black hole collisions, plus neutron star collisions.

LIGO and future detectors will help us understand events in deep space that were previously unknown to us. Not only will we learn more about black holes and neutron stars, but we also may be able to hear the beginning of the universe, the Big Bang. Of course, scientists will also be listening for unknown signals that may reveal surprising—and maybe even shocking!—results.

Author's Note

I watched a livestream of the LIGO news conference on February 11, 2016, anticipating the announcement of the discovery of gravitational waves. My excitement doubled when Gaby González stepped up to the podium to speak. I was truly inspired to see a Latina scientist announcing this monumental discovery. Since that day, Gaby has been one of my role models. I hope she inspires others as well.

Timeline

1879: Albert Einstein is born in Ulm, Germany, on March 14, 1879.

1915: Einstein finishes his general theory of relativity.

1916: Einstein publishes a paper predicting the existence of gravitational waves.

1921: Einstein is awarded the Nobel Prize in Physics.

1955: Einstein dies on April 18, 1955, in Princeton, New Jersey.

1965: Gabriela (Gaby) González is born in Córdoba, Argentina, on February 24, 1965.

1988: González graduates from the University of Córdoba with a degree in physics.

1989: González moves to Syracuse, New York.

1994: Construction of LIGO begins.

1997: González joins the LIGO team.

2011: González becomes the LIGO spokesperson.

2015: First detection of gravitational waves by LIGO.

2016: As spokesperson for the LIGO team, González helps announce the discovery to the world.

2017: González is awarded the Bruno Rossi Prize and the National Academy of Sciences Award for Scientific Discovery.

Glossary

Black hole: A dense area of space with intense gravitational pull; even light cannot escape the gravity of a black hole.

Gravitational waves: Ripples in space-time caused by a high-energy event such as the collision of two black holes; theorized by Albert Einstein in 1916 and detected by LIGO in 2015.

Interferometer: An instrument that creates interference patterns of light waves to make very small measurements.

LIGO: Laser Interferometer Gravitational-Wave Observatory; detected the first gravitational wave on September 14, 2015.

Neutron star: A highly dense star formed from the collapse of giant stars; gravity on a neutron star is two billion times stronger than gravity on Earth.

Space-time: The three dimensions of space (length, width, and depth), plus a fourth dimension of time, in which objects exist.

Thermal noise: Electronic noise caused when free electrons are agitated by heat; thermal noise can interfere with the detection of gravitational waves.

Selected Sources

Abbott, B. P., et al. (LIGO Scientific Collaboration and Virgo Collaboration). "Characterization of Transient Noise in Advanced LIGO Relevant to Gravitational Wave Signal GW150914." *Classical and Quantum Gravity,* June 6, 2016. 33, 134001.

Abbott B. P., et al. (LIGO Scientific Collaboration and Virgo Collaboration). "Observation of Gravitational Waves from a Binary Black Hole Merger." *Physical Review Letters,* February 11, 2016. 116, 061102.

Castelvecchi, Davide. "*Nature*'s 10: Ten People Who Mattered This Year; Gabriela González: Gravity Spy." *Nature,* December 19, 2016.

Castelvecchi, Davide, and Alexandra Witze. "Einstein's Gravitational Waves Found at Last." *Nature,* February 11, 2016.

Kruesi, Liz. "Searching the Sky for the Wobbles of Gravity." *Quanta Magazine,* October 22, 2015. Web. 21, April 2017.

Overbye, Dennis. "With Faint Chirp, Scientists Prove Einstein Correct." *The New York Times,* February 12, 2016. A1.

Videos

ligo.caltech.edu/video/ligo01032005v
("Einstein's Messengers," a documentary about LIGO's search for gravitational waves)

worldsciencefestival.com/videos/pioneers-science-gabriela-gonzalez-english/
(A short profile of Gaby González and her work on the LIGO project)

Websites

ligo.caltech.edu
(The main LIGO page from Caltech University; links to LIGO Livingston and LIGO Hanford; includes educational resources)

ligo.org/index.php
(The LIGO Scientific Collaboration website; includes educational resources)

ligo.org/magazine/LIGO-magazine-issue-8-extended.pdf
(The March 2016 edition of *LIGO Magazine*, dedicated to the first detection of gravitational waves)

news.syr.edu/blog/2019/01/04/physicist-gabriela-gonzalez-g95-reveals-how-syracuse-prepared-her-to
-make-science-history/
(Syracuse University interview with Gaby González)

spaceplace.nasa.gov/gravitational-waves/en
(NASA website describing gravitational waves for kids)

wbur.org/hereandnow/2016/06/14/profile-scientist-gravitational-waves
(A short audio interview with Gaby González)

www.phys.lsu.edu/faculty/gonzalez
(Gaby González's personal homepage)

light detector → light waves

light waves hit the light detector

bound...

curvature of space

laser

$$G_{\alpha\beta} = \frac{8\pi G}{c^4} T_{\mu\nu}$$

$$h = 2G \frac{1}{c^4} \frac{1}{r} \frac{\partial^2 Q}{\partial t^2}$$

some constants

power recycling mirror

← beam splitter

test mass

$$h = 2G \frac{1}{c^4} \frac{1}{r} \frac{\partial^2 Q}{\partial t^2}$$

Ripples in space

$$\left[\nabla^2 - \frac{1}{c^2} \frac{\partial^2}{\partial t^2} \right] h_{\mu\nu} = 0$$

beam spl...

light